D0115946

To misunderstood penguins everywhere . . .

Deepest gratitude to my agent, Michelle, and Emma and Josh at
Headline for believing in my misbehaving penguins, and to my other
half, whose trust in my craziness has made this book possible.

First published in 2008 by Simon Spotlight Entertainment,
an imprint of Simon & Schuster Inc

First published in the United Kingdom in 2008 by
HEADLINE PUBLISHING GROUP

2

Cataloguing in Publication Data is available from the British Library

ISBN 978 0 7553 1804 9

Typeset by Avon DataSet Ltd, Bidford-on-Avon, Warwickshire

Printed in the UK by CPI William Clowes Beccles NR34 7TL

Headline's policy is to use papers that are natural, renewable and
recyclable products and made from wood grown in sustainable
forests. The logging and manufacturing processes are expected to
conform to the environmental regulations of the country of origin.

HEADLINE PUBLISHING GROUP
An Hachette Livre UK Company
338 Euston Road
London NW1 3BH

www.headline.co.uk
www.hachettelivre.co.uk
www.evil-penguins.co.uk
www.evilpenguinnews.com

THE 11th PLAGUE: PENGUINS

MARCH OF THE PENGUINS

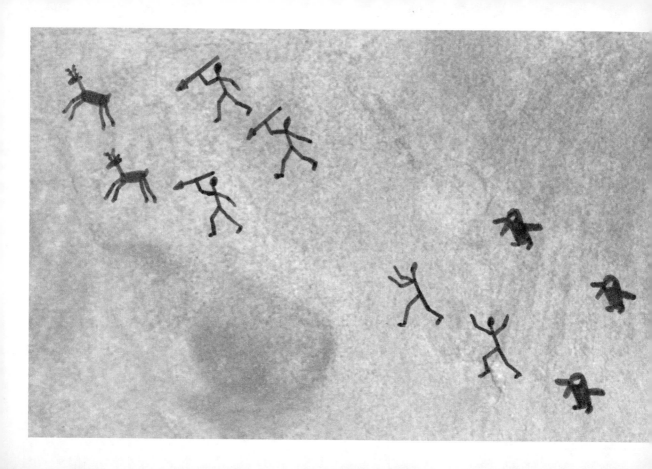

The Chinese Empire defends against the barbarian hordes from Antarctica.

ANIMAL TESTING

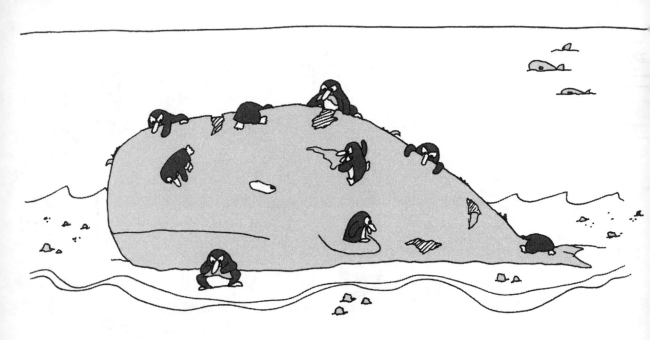

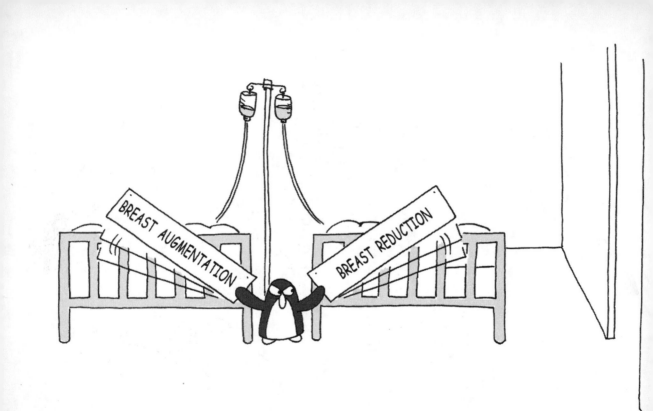

KOALA ON THE BARBIE

TROJAN PENGUIN

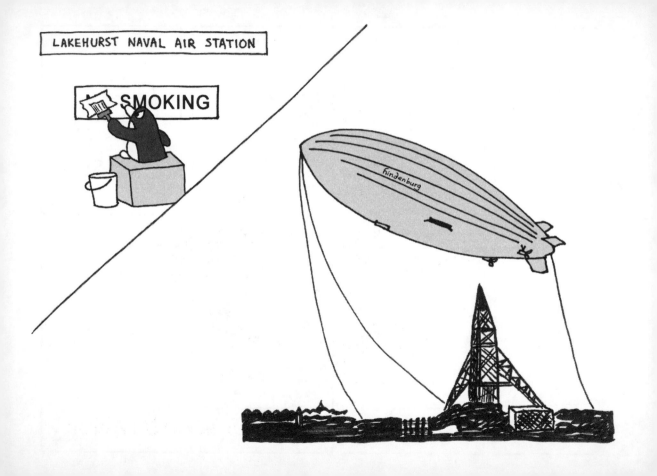

PEKING PANDA (ORDER 24 HRS IN ADVANCE)

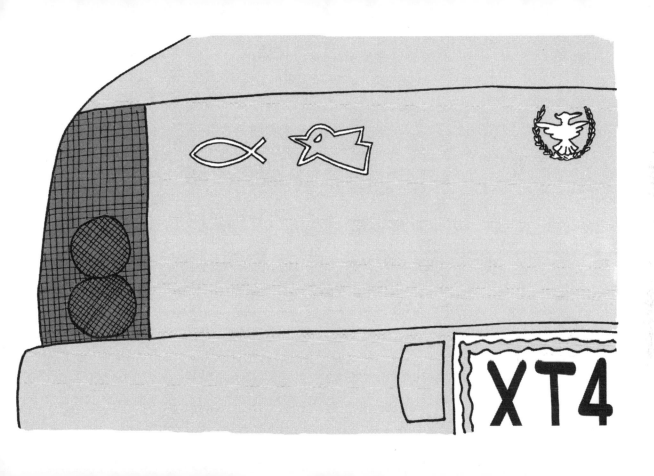

LIQUID: a state of matter which assumes the shape of its container, while retaining its volume